Tattered Woman

A Precious Soul Indeed

Courtney J. Hansen

BookLeaf Publishing

India | USA | UK

Made with ❤ on the BookLeaf Publishing Platform
www.bookleafpub.in
www.bookleafpub.com

Dedication

To every woman who has ever had love go terribly wrong.

Preface

Domestic violence and sexual assault are real problems that people deal with and they are often left in the shadows. I hope that these poems can help to express some of the difficult feelings and experiences of those who have been hurt by those who should have loved them. Each survivor of domestic violence and sexual assault has their own unique story, but we can find comfort, strength, and healing in one another as we bring our stories out of the shadows and into the light. These poems, while not directly tied to any one individual, are inspired by real individuals who I have witnessed rise from the ashes of broken homes. For many survivors, leaving their abuser is difficult for various reasons, and is a process of individuals regaining autonomy and learning to recognize patterns of abuse. Isolation is a major factor in keeping victims trapped in unhealthy relationships and gives the abuser power to control and manipulate. Please know that you are never alone. The National Hotline is always available and there are many resources out there to help in whatever situation you may find yourself. Their number is: 800-799-7233

Acknowledgements

I would like to acknowledge my dear friends who have opened up their hearts to share with me their experiences of broken love, domestic violence, and sexual assault. Their experiences break my heart, but I hope that we can all be more aware of how to help and become more empathetic to those who have suffered or still suffer from abuse.

1. Tattered Woman

Tattered woman, where are you?
I've been searching far too long.
You're wanted here, and oh, so loved
I yearn to hear your song.

Tattered woman, please come home
I'll hold you in warm embrace.
your pain and hurt, to me are known
I'll heal you with my grace.

Tattered woman have some hope
Your story's not yet done.
The heart inside your chest is broke
A Jewel you will become.

2. The Walls Stand Broken

The walls stand broken
A flash of anger, then a scar
The walls stand broken
How do I know it's gone too far?

The walls stand broken
Our home's become a place of fear
The walls stand broken
If only I could disappear

The walls stand broken
How oft I send the kids to play
The walls stand broken
I know they're safe, if they're away

The walls stand broken
It's not so bad, I speak a lie
The walls stand broken
I touch my tender, bloody eye

The walls stand broken

3. He Holds Me

He holds me with an iron grip
A grip once gentle and kind
A grip without a chance to slip
No where he will not find

He holds my voice, I dare not speak
for fear I'll lose my mind
A fool could see his poison leak
Perhaps I'm truly blind

My confidence has been misplaced
My courage left behind
I'm trapped inside his cruel embrace
A trap that he designed

The Joy, the pain, the love, the hate
are completely intertwined
The reality in which I live
Is one that he defined

4. Little Princess

Little Princess, destined a queen
Little Princess, a future unseen
Little Princess, Smile so bright
Little Princess, scatter your light

Little Princess, grow big and strong
Little Princess, who does no wrong
Little Princess, who loves to play
Little Princess, grows up one day

Little Princess, kind and sweet
Little Princess, the world mistreats
Little Princess, good looks a curse
Little Princess, they do their worst

Little Princess, becomes a slave
Little Princess, dreams of the grave
Little Princess, by morning weeps
Little Princess, she rarely sleep

Little Princess, her voice not heard
Little Princess, don't be absurd
Little Princess, we should protect
A Promise Made, but then unkept

5. Determined

I know that I'll be healed one day
when my hurt has said what it needs to say
I will stand tall with my head held high
once I have cried all the tears in my eye

I will be strong, stronger than before
when my heavy heart is done being so sore
I will laugh again, I may not show it
When my fears don't force me to stay so quiet

I will learn to play, to dance and sing
once these memories have lost their sting
I will be happy, believe me or not
I'll remember how, or I'll be retaught

6. Years of my Youth

This might be it for me...
A blossom bloomed and spent
My past is faded memory
My future came and went

The days of youth I gave away
Like a fool I gave to you
My living breath, you stole from me
You turned me black and blue

A woman should age, graced with love
But I was graced with pain
My wrinkles aren't from smiling dear
They were carved by my eyes rain

7. Never satisfied

Words words words
You never know what to say
Whether its kind or mean; soft' or loud
It's wrong, in every way

Clothes clothes clothes
You never know what to wear
It shows to much or not enough
It always earns his glare

Meals meals meals
You never know what to fix
A five star meal, or covered in mold
He'll give you several kicks

Chores chores chores
You never know what needs done
You work all day on this and that
He'll still threaten you just for fun

Time time time
You never know how to spend
Give it to him, or stay away
He always claims it's end

8. Fortress prison

I spent a lifetime building a fortress to keep my heart
from breaking
For I was so young when I learned of it's fragility
If I'd known of its need for the sun and sky
Perhaps I would have built a window

Who knew I'd be the evil witch of my own story
Locking all that was good within me, high in a tower
Untouchable but longing to be touched
To be seen, heard, wanted, desired

I failed you young maiden, I left you hungry
So hungry when our eyes met his it was like looking in a
mirror
And you thought it was love
But the hungry can't feed the hungry

His embrace felt safe, for you were used to being tied up
in chains
You knew no different
I taught you no different

The world had been cruel to us, so I tried to make you invisible
But he saw you, those dazzling bewitching eyes
Saw into the depths of your lonely soul
Impressive as a bird of prey

He's charming, but it's a lie, he offers only fools gold
Be brave and believe you are a princess worthy of a real prince
Not a thief, not a frog, not a beast, not an injured soul only you can fix
Be kind, but let them pass

Do not be the maiden in distress, needing to be rescued
Learn to love and be loved back.
To be grateful and strong
Find the one to match your goodness
Who gives and gladly receives
Rather than takes and is never satisfied

Go run from this tower that I have built and find your prince
Beware of impostures who always come
Once they reveal themselves, let them go
True love is sacrifice
Believe that you will find someone worthy of your love
So that your sacrifice be not vain

9. My choice

The stars, the moon, the sun the sky
they seem to stay the same to me, but I
I am not the same

The mountains eroding with the wind
The leaves evolve and change their skin
These are my kin

We dissolve, adapt, accommodate
shifting shapes to keep us safe
from the tyrannical elements that engulf us.

We have no wings to take up flight
possess no strength to stand and fight
so we change

In one small thing we're not alike
My change has choice for what I like
So I learn

10. head unbowed

She stands tall in her care worn gown
As if it were a new
Her story woven by each thread
Emboldened by her truth

The darkened stains upon her knee
Left from the time she crawled
Through fire and ash of broken love
When words were used to scald

The faded print tells of the days
Filled with hate and strife
Faded by the angry rays
Of what should have given life

Her smile now does brighten all
Bringing color to her cheeks
She is a gem so beautiful
That all the wise now seek

11. Scorched

Does the desert cry at night?
Or does she collapse after the many
heated fights of the day?
Perhaps she is past feeling and beyond caring

If she does cry, where do her tears go?
Surely her heart is to hard to let them sink more
than skin deep?

Her protection has become offensive
to strike first and be deadly
Trust is something too green to survive
In her harsh world

As quickly as it sprouts it is scorched
Singed at the tears in her precious and thirsty soul
She lives a different life, a dangerous life, a lonely life

Her hardened skin, like armor
Has grown accustomed to take the beating stripes
Of the blistering sun

She reclaims her power the only way she knows
And no longer burns because she rid herself

Of all things flammable

No she does not cry at night
Rather she guards her precious tears
With long, sharp cactus thorns and venom's fangs

Ready to tear the flesh of any and all who try to set them
free
Friend or foe
She has yet to learn the difference

Her thirst for love is far too disorienting to be able to
figure it out
For even the gentle caress of a soft starlit night
Feels so extreme against her cheek

If to heal is to hurt
And to continue on is to hurt
Then perhaps it really is best to hold still

Safest to hold her breath
As if to hold time itself...

Not a rise or fall of her chest
Or a whisper of escaping air
But perfect stillness...

Her apathy is a mirage

For the sun still rises and the sun still sets
And will forever, until she learns from her own
experience
Which pain hurts
And which pain heals
And then chooses to be healed

12. I love you still

I loved you, I still love you
I stayed because I thought you'd love me back
the way you once did, do you remember?

Do you remember when first we met?
You showed me so much love
I guess to you I was your pet
Vulnerable as a dove

Do you remember when you took me out
To a world I'd never seen?
Now you hit, you scream, and shout
Destroying what was our dream

Do you remember the words you spoke?
So lovely and kind they were
Safely conned, 'til I awoke
To a life filled with despair

I loved you once, I love you still
A dangerous thing I know
Your frigid heart gives a deadly chill
That's why I now must go

13. Leaving

I'm waiting, waiting to fly
His anger is kindled, his mercy has dwindled
but I always refuse to die

I'm prepared, prepared to run
I know that I'm frightened, my senses are heightened
but I know where he keeps the gun

I'm ready, ready to go
the bags are packed, my soul is racked
and I pray he doesn't know

I'm leaving, leaving for real
whatever my fate, he is much too late
because I no longer feel

I'm hiding, hiding for now
If he finds me, I'm dead, at least that's what he said
His victory I won't allow

I'm healing, healing today
I know I was hurt, treated like dirt
reshaped like potters clay

I'm breathing, breathing again
One step at a time, I'm making the climb
until the day that I win

14. Born lucky

Some are born into families with an abundance of love
others are born into families that leave a gnawing in
their heart
A hunger not easy to fill, for the world takes pleasure to
rob and steal

Some can see through the lies of a maleficent foe,
because they know
others are blind by the throbbing of their soul
for...something
A deep need to be loved, they think its normal when
they're beaten and shoved

Some know they are worth more than rubies, diamonds,
and gold
others believe they are less than the dirt, and it hurts
so they bend over backwards at a chance to prove
something they don't believe

15. Confession

This is my confession, I am his possession
a point of contention, with zero protection from he
I blame his depression, for all his aggression
He'll teach me a lesson, if not to perfection I be

His angry obsession, has cost our connection
no room for affection, or place of expression from me
no need for inspection, he gives this impression
for no one to question, a man of destruction he be

16. Warrior

I look in the mirror and what do I see?
A woman much stronger and wiser than me
She has such fire and emotional grit
In the depths of despair she never did quit

She smiles and tells me that I'll be alright
She will protect me and hold me so tight
Others avoid her, her gaze is so stern
I am so grateful she knows to be firm

When I'm in danger, she draws her sword
And fights my battles with little reward
Her armor is heavy, but always with-holds
Deflects and protects from enemy's blows

Behind her strong smile, the glint in her eye
You'll feel her longing, and hunger to fly
To soar as an eagle, away from this world
Relieved of her duty, a white flag unfurled

17. Get out

Get out of my life, you aren't welcome here
Much damage you've done, but no longer I fear
This space in my life, you cannot afford
I'm kicking you out, that's your reward
For hurting my body, with your angry fist
I did nothing wrong, you were just pissed
I loved you so dearly, and treated you kindly
but I will no longer trust you so blindly
I've learned so much from the time that I spent
"Earning" your love, while I paid the rent
I learned that true love is not to be earned
And by ones actions true love is confirmed
Because of your violence, I've grown some thick skin
So stay far away from me and my kin

18. My Mind Was Stolen

I don't want to decide, at least not about what I want
Making a choice intimidates me, and knowing my
desires is painful
All of my choices have been made for me for so long
now my life's a mess and I have to decide, between bad
and worse
How is that fair? Now that I question everything, and
everyone
What are my options? Do I even have any?
They seem quite scarce now that I'm on my own
I don't know what to do. How could I?
My mind was stolen
Can I delegate and have someone decide for me?
I've been handed freedom and I don't know what to do
with it
Tell me what I'm supposed to do, I'll do that. I know how
to fit a mold
My previous slave master went from good to bad
but perhaps a new one would treat me better
Then I could put on a new skin, and be safe
Safe from being my own, I could never be responsible
enough
love myself enough, be patient enough
I need someone else to tell me who I am, where to go,

how to be
Surely I am unqualified to define myself
will someone do it for me? please?

19. I feel nothing

I feel nothing, not the warmth of the sun
nor the chill of the night
The pain became far too great
So I shut up, and then shut down

Till I felt nothing

Anger's hot breath has left me this time
It came so fast, but left so slow
Love's fragile frame is shattered
pieces scattered and lost
I care not to find them

For I feel nothing

Your voice is loud and sharp, meant to pierce my heart
and kill my spirit, but I've been dead a long long while
so do your worst, anything worth losing I've already lost

So I feel nothing

20. Invisible Murder

There are no words
For the deep betrayal of the one I loved the most
The Horror of realizing I gave Him everything
I trusted him to keep it safe
There are not words for what I feel
When my heart remembers what I fool I was
Robbed of the purest and deepest love it could ever know
for someone else
Love now, forever tainted. Never will it bloom again
The most sacred space within my soul
Now stands desecrated
By your cruel and careless foot prints

And I screamed. And I screamed. And I screamed

For the girl I was, so cheerful and bright is now dead.
Murdered by her first love, a pawn in his twisted game
She will be used no more, but I am left to try to fill her
place
Using her memory to remember how to act
In the lives of all those who loved her
And I grieve her death alone
While you, you walk away, her blood dripping
From the knife you hold in your hand

Invisible but to God and me
Her spirit is gone, and you walk free
For who would believe her dead
When her body still walks and breaths
And blood flows in her veins?

21. A New Dawn

A new dawn came, I'm not the same
I feel it in the air
Bees are buzzing, birds are humming
The squirrels, they stop and stare

I'm shy at first, I've seen the worst
Now the sun peaks over the hills
Like the rising sun, I've finally won
O'er the nights that caused such chills

In the crisp cool morning, new dreams are forming
For the day that's yet to be
I let out a sigh for all the days gone by
They are now only history

The ground frost melts, like pain once felt
On each tender blade of grass
The golden rays of bright hope's gaze
Lands on my face at last